I0554982

THE EIGHT VICES

Eutropius of Valencia

Bishop of Valencia

Translated by: D.P. Curtin

Dalcassian
Publishing
Company

PHILADELPHIA, PA

ISBN: 978-1-960069-83-2 (Paperback)

Library of Congress Control Number:
Author: Curtin, D.P. (1985-)

Printed by Ingram Content Group, 1 Ingram Blvd, La Vergne, Tennessee

First printing edition 2017.

Introduction

The cult of saints is an imprecise science when it comes to the Dark Ages. There seems to be an endless parade of unknown saints that briefly held pious prominence, only to be forgotten within a generation. Eutropius of Valencia is a peer in this college of forgotten holymen. Some Spanish records grant him the title of saint, but most do not. The authority for granting this prefix in the 7th century was ill-defined. Nevertheless, during his tenure as the bishop of Valencia, he attempted to shepherd his flock with a treatise on vice and virtue. Most of his work is a reiteration of the virtue ethics that were strongly encouraged in the classical world. However, the era that he lived in was not one renowned for its moral order or restraint. Visigothic Spain was precariously on the edge of collapse, with its regular civil wars and its loose sense of governance over its own subjects. The church was able to impose on society what little order it could, and this included an education on establishing good and bad behaviors.

Based on the nature and style of his writings, Eutropius may have been influenced by the Gallic churchman, John Cassian, who held similar views regarding the nature of morality. Eutropius starts to outline the similarities that exist between the vices and how their commonalities can be used to classify their explicit danger. His work on the subject serves as one of the steppingstones between classical virtue ethics and the systemic morality that was developed by the Thomistic school in the Middle Ages.

D.P. Curtin
May 31, 2017
Pittsburgh, PA

There are eight principal vices which afflict the human race.

First, there is gastrimargia (gut-madness), which sounds like a sinking of the stomach. Second; fornication. Thirdly, philargyry, that is avarice, or the love of money. The fourth is anger. The fifth is depression. The sixth is acedia, that is, anxiety or weariness of the heart. Seventhly, cenodoxia, that is, boasting or vainglory. The eighth is pride. Therefore, these are the eight vices, and although they have different origins and difficult efficiencies, the prior six, that is, gastrimargia, fornication, philargy, anger, sadness, apathy, are connected with each other by a kind of kinship and, as I might say, concatenation. So that the exuberance of the former becomes the beginning of the following.

For, from the abundance of gastrimargia, it is necessary to breed fornication, from fornication philanthropy, from philanthropy anger, from anger sadness, from sadness acidity. Therefore, we must fight against these things in the same way and with the same reason, and we must always enter into a struggle against those things which have gone before, and those who follow after. Therefore, in order to overcome apathy, sadness must be overcome. In order that sadness may be driven away, anger must be extinguished. And for that anger to be extinguished, philargy must be trampled upon, Now, in order that philargy may rise, immorality must be checked, and so that fornication may be overthrown, the vice of gastritis must be punished. Yet, the remaining two, that is, cenodoxia and pride, are indeed joined to themselves in the same way as that which we have said of the former, so that the growth of the former becomes the rise of the latter. Cenodoxia gives birth to the fuel of excessive pride. For when those six are uprooted, these two bear fruit more vigorously than when they are dead, and these sprout and grow more vigorously. Hence, we are attacked by these two in a different way.

We fell into each one of those six vices when we were eluded by the previous ones. In these two cases, even the victors are in danger after their triumphs.

For these eight vices which we have mentioned are divided into four conjugations and copulas. For gastrimargia and fornication are united by a special union, and in like manner, so are philargy with anger. Sadness and acedia are also connected by the same conjunction. Cenodoxia, too, and pride are intimately connected with themselves. You have heard the couplings, now hear the types of vices.

There are three types of gastritis. The first one is the kind that comes before the canonical hour the Christian continues to eat. Secondly, from the superfluity of any food or drink, in which the people of Israel sinned when they made the golden calf, as it is written (Exodus 32). Therefore, the people sat down to eat and drink, and rose up to play. The third, that he longed for the finest and most delicate foods. It was this one that the sons of Eli sinned, who refused to accept cooked meat from the people, but raw, so that they might more carefully prepare it for themselves (1 Kings 2). From these three kinds strange and horrible diseases of the soul are produced. From the first: anger for those who had to prepare the food, from the second: a sting of lust and desire is raised, and the third: the bindings of the inextricable snares of philargyry around the necks of the captives.

There are three kinds of fornication: First, there is thought, of which the Lord says in the Gospel (Matthew 5): "He who sees a woman and has lust in his heart, and the rest"; secondly, that it is accomplished by the conjunction of both sexes; the third, without the touch of a woman, which the Apostle calls impurity (Gal. 5). These three things are to be guarded against with equal observance by us, lest any one of these deter and exclude us from the kingdom of Christ.

There are three kinds of philargy: the first is that it does not allow a person to be despoiled of superfluous resources. This was the sin of (Acts 5) Ananias and Sapphira. According to the fact that he persuades with greater desire to resume what has been scattered by us to the needy. Judas fell into this fault, who sold the Lord. Thirdly, being forced to desire or acquire those things which we did not possess before. In this Gehazi sinned.

There are three kinds of anger: one that burns inwardly and is unable to speak because of indignation. Yet, another, which breaks out into word and deed and effect. The third, which is reserved for days and times.

There are two kinds of sadness: one that is generated by ending anger from a loss inflicted or from a longing that has been hindered, and another which descends from reasonable mental anxiety or despair.

There are two kinds of acedia: the one which precipitates to the top those who are warm, otherwise, he is neither pleased to do good or hear good. Such as with those who might throw a monk out of his cell.

Cenodoxia, although it is manifold and multiform and is divided into different species, yet there are two kinds of it: the first is that which is emphasized for carnal and manifest things, and the secondly, that for spiritual and secret desires. We are inflamed with vain praise.

There are two kinds of pride: first, carnal, and secondly, spiritual, which is even more destructive. For [the devil] attacks more acutely those whom he finds advanced in certain virtues. You have heard the genera and conjunction and concatenation; hear now what kind of daughters they have that are born from them.

For from gastrimargia are born lunatic fits and drunkenness; of fornication, obscenities, scurrilities, amusements, and foolish talk; of philargyry, lying, cheating, perjury, lust for profit, false witness, violence, inhumanity and rapacity; of anger, murders, clamor and indignation; of sadness, rancor, pusillanimity, bitterness, despair; of apathy, atrocity, sleepiness, importunity, restlessness, wandering, instability of mind and body, talkativeness and curiosity; of cenodoxia, contentions, heresies, boasting and presumption of innovations; of pride, contempt, envy, disobedience, blasphemy, murmuring, and detraction. These, then, are the eight vices, when they affect the race of men, yet they do not affect them all in one way. For in another the spirit of fornication occupies the principal place, and in another, fury prevails. In another, cenodoxia vindicates tyranny. In another, pride holds a fortress. And since it is clear that everyone is attacked by everything, we each work in a different way and order.

Wherefore we must fight against these things in such a way that each one explores the vice with which he is most infested and takes up the main struggle against it. For even the law giver (Deut. 7) teaches us in these words that we ought to exercise one order of battle and not to rely on our own strength: "You shall not be afraid of them, for the Lord your God is in your midst, a great and terrible God. He will consume these nations in your sight little by little and bit by bit. You will not be able to destroy them together, lest the beasts of the earth multiply against you, and the Lord your God will give them in your sight until they are completely destroyed. But neither ought we to be exalted in their victories", as he warns (Deut. 8): "Lest after you have eaten, he says, and are satisfied, and have built beautiful houses and lived in them, and have herds and flocks of sheep, silver and gold, and abundance of all things, let your heart be lifted up. Yet, you will not remember the Lord your God, who brought you out of the land of Egypt, from the house of slavery, and was your guide in the great and terrible wilderness." Solomon also in Proverbs (Prov. 24): "If your enemy has fallen, do not congratulate yourself, but in supplanting him do not exaggerate. Let not his lord see and turn away his wrath from him. That is to say, lest you should dissipate the elation of your heart, it should depart from its attack, and you should begin leaving it behind, to be tormented again by that passion which you had overcome by the grace of God."

Wherefore, it befits us to be sure, both of the facts themselves and of the innumerable testimonies of the Scriptures, that we cannot overcome so many enemies by our own strength, unless we are supported by the help of God alone, and that we must daily refer to him the sum of our victory. Thus, also through Moses (Deut. 9), reminding the Lord: "Do not say in your heart, when the Lord your God has destroyed them before your eyes 'Because of my righteousness the Lord brought me in to possess this land, when because of their impiety they became destroyed nations. For you will not go in to possess their land because of your righteousness and the equity of your heart, but because they acted impiously when you entered, and therefore they were destroyed'". I ask what could have been said more openly, or more cautiously? With what caution we must be!

These are the seven nations whose lands the Lord promises to give to the children of Israel after they came out of Egypt. All this, according to the Apostle, when it happened to them in figure, we must receive it written out for our admonition (Deut. 7).

For it is said: "When the Lord God brought you into the land which you would possess, and destroyed many nations before you, the Hittites, the Gergezaites, the Amorites, the Canaanites, the Perizzites, the Jebusites, and the Nevaites, seven nations far greater in number and stronger than you. You and the Lord shall deliver them unto you, and smite them to the point of extermination."

The reason why they are said to be a much greater number is because there are more vices than virtues. And therefore, seven nations are indeed enumerated in the catalog. Yet, in the conquest they are placed without the inscription of numbers. For thus it is said: "And he shall destroy many nations before thee. For the people of carnal passions are more numerous than Israel, which proceeds from this seventh fuel and root of vices, and from the eighth", which is better known to all, the queen and the mother of all vices. For from these eight, these daughters spring up and are born, that is to say: debauchery, drunkenness, obscenity, etc., described above, which is too long to mention. Let us hear what the apostle felt about them (2 Cor. 10), or what his opinion was about them: "You shall not murmur," says he, "as some of them murmured, and perished by the exterminator." And about the temptation: "Let us not tempt Christ, as some of them were tempted and perished from serpents." On withdrawal: "Do not love to withdraw, lest you be uprooted" and several others similar to these. Although these things are much greater in number than the virtues, yet having conquered those eight principal vices, from whose nature it is certain that they emanate, they all immediately cease, and are destroyed together with them in perpetual extermination.

In fact, as far as the old tradition teaches, these same lands of the Canaanites into which the children of Israel were introduced, had once been allotted to Shem, the sons of Noah, in the division of the world. Afterwards, by force and power, the posterity of Ham possessed the iniquity of persuasion, in which the most just judgment of God is confirmed. He also drove them out of the foreign lands which they had wrongfully occupied, and restored to them the ancient possession of their fathers which had been allotted to their descendants in the division of the world. It is known with a very certain reason that this figure also stands in us. For the Lord's will naturally deputed the possession of our heart not to vices, but to virtues. Which, after the transgression of Adah, by unaccustomed vices, that is, the Canaanite peoples, driven from their own country, when they were again restored to them by the grace of God, our diligence and labor, did not so much occupy foreign lands as they are supposed to have recovered their own.

Solomon also describes this seven-fold fuel of vices in Proverbs (Prov. 26): "If an enemy asks you with a loud voice, you will not agree to him", for there are seven iniquities in his soul. That is, if the gastrimargia persuades you to relax the body, which you have just decided on continence, do not loosen its subjection, because immediately seven spirits of vices will come to you, more acute than that passion which had been overcome at the beginning, and they will soon drag you into worse kinds of vices. Therefore, the Lord is to be implored in all things, that his mercy may help us where our strength is not.

LATIN TEXT

De octo vitiis

Octo sunt vitia principalia quae humanum genus infestant.

Primum, gastrimargia, quod sonat ventris ingluvies; secundum; fornicatio; tertium, philargyria, id est avaritia, sive amor pecuniae; quartum, ira, quintum; tristitia; sextum, acedia, id est anxietas sive taedium cordis; septimum, cenodoxia, id est jactantia seu vana gloria; octavum, superbia. Haec igitur octo vitia, licet diversos ortus ac difficiles efficientias habeant, sex tamen priora, id est, gastrimargia, fornicatio, philargyria, ira, tristitia, acedia, quadam inter se cognatione et, ut dixerim, concatenatione, connexa sunt. Ita ut prioris exuberantia sequentium efficiatur exordium.

Nam de abundantia gastrimargiae fornicationem, de fornicatione philargyriam, de philargyria iram, de ira tristitiam, de tristitia acediam, necesse est pullulare. Ideoque simili contra haec modo atque eadem ratione pugnandum est, et praecedentium semper adversus sequentes oportet nos inire certamen. Quamobrem, ut acedia vincatur, superanda est tristitia; ut tristitia propellatur, ira exstinguenda est; ut exstinguatur ira, philargyria conculcanda; ut evallatur philargyria, fornicatio compescenda est; ut fornicatio subruatur, gastrimargiae vitium est castigandum. Residuae vero duae, id est, cenodoxia et superbia sibi quidem similiter illa qua de superioribus diximus ratione junguntur, ita ut incrementum prioris ortus efficiatur alterius. Cenodoxiae exsuperantia superbiae fomitem parit. Nam illis sex evulsis, haec duo vehementius fructificant, et illis mortuis, vivacius istae pullulant et succrescunt. Unde et diverso modo ab his duobus impugnamur.

In unumquodque illorum sex vitiorum tunc incidimus cum a praecedentibus illorum fuerimus elisi. In his vero duobus etiam victores post triumphos periclitamur.

Nam et ista octo vitia quae commemoravimus in quatuor conjugationes et copulas dividuntur. Gastrimargia namque et fornicatio peculiari consortio foederantur, simili modo philargyria cum ira. Tristitia quoque et acedia eadem copulatione junguntur. Cenodoxia quoque atque superbia familiariter et ipsa sibi conjunguntur. Audivisti copulationes, audi nunc genera vitiorum.

Gastrimargiae genera sunt tria. Primum quod ante horam canonicam perurget Christianum comedere: in hac peccavit Jonathan, filius Saul, irrumpens juramentum patris, unde nec victoriam meruit populus de inimicis habere; secundum, ex quarumlibet escarum vel potus superfluitate, in qua peccavit populus Israeliticus cum fabricavit vitulum aureum, sicut scriptum est (Exod. XXXII): Sedit populus manducare et bibere, et surrexerunt ludere; tertium, quod accuratiores et delicatissimos cibos desideret. In hoc peccaverunt filii Heli qui noluerunt carnem coctam accipere a populo, sed crudam, ut diligentius sibi praepararent (I Reg. II). Ex his tribus generibus diversae et pessimae valetudines animae procreantur. Nam de primo ira illi qui parare cibum debuit, de secundo luxuriae ac libidinis aculei suscitantur; tertium autem inextricabiles philargyriae laqueos nectit cervicibus captivorum.

Fornicationis genera tria sunt: Primum, cogitatio est, de qua Dominus ita in Evangelio (Matth. V) dicit: Qui viderit mulierem ad concupiscendam eam, et caetera; secundum, quod per commistionem sexus utriusque perficitur; tertium, absque feminae tactu, quod Apostolus immunditiam (Gal. IV) nuncupat. Quae tria sic sunt a nobis pari observatione cavenda, ne a regno Christi unumquodlibet horum nos deterreat et excludat.

Philargyriae genera sunt tria: primum quod exspoliari non sinit hominem facultatibus superfluis, in hoc peccaverunt (Act. V) Ananias et Sapphira; secundum quod ea quae a nobis dispersa sunt indigentibus, cum majori cupiditate persuadet resumere: in hanc culpam incidit Judas, qui Dominum vendidit; tertium quod ea quae ante non possedimus infrunite desiderari vel acquiri compellimur. In hac peccavit Giezi.

Irae genera sunt tria: unum quod exardescit intrinsecus et prae indignatione non valet loqui; aliud, quod in verbum et opus effectumque prorumpit; tertium, quod per dies et tempora reservatur.

Tristitiae genera sunt duo: unum quod ira desinente de illato damno vel desiderio praepedito generatur; aliud quod de rationabili mentis anxietate seu desperatione descendit.

Acediae sunt genera duo: unum quod ad summum praecipitat aestuantes; aliud quo nec bonum facere nec audire delectat. Ista ejicit monachum de cella sua.

Cenodoxia, licet multiplex ac multiformis est et in diversas species dividitur, genera tamen ejus sunt duo: primum quod pro carnalibus ac manifestis extollitur rebus; secundum, quod pro spiritualibus et occultis desideriis vanae laudis inflamur.

Superbiae genera sunt duo: primum, carnale; secundum, spirituale, quod etiam perniciosius est. Illos namque specialius impugnat quos in quibusdam virtutibus profecisse reperit. Audisti genera et conjunctionem atque concatenationem, audi nunc quales habeant filias quae de eis nascuntur.

De gastrimargia namque nascuntur comessationes, ebrietates; de fornicatione, turpiloquia, scurrilitates, ludicra ac stultiloquia; de philargyria, mendacium, fraudatio, perjuria, turpis lucri appetitus, falsa tesmonia, violentia, inhumanitas ac rapacitas; de ira, homicidia, clamor et indignatio; de tristitia, rancor, pusillanimitas, amaritudo, desperatio; de acedia, atrocitas, somnolentia, importunitas, inquietudo, pervagatio, instabilitas mentis et corporis, verbositas et curiositas; de cenodoxia, contentiones, haereses, jactantia ac praesumptio novitatum; de superbia, contemptus, invidia, inobedientia, blasphemia, murmuratio atque detractio. Haec igitur octa vitia sunt, cum hominum genus impulsent, non tamen uno modo impetunt cunctos. In alio namque spiritus fornicationum locum obtinet principalem. In alio superequitat furor. In alio cenodoxia vindicat tyrannidem. In alio arcem superbia tenet. Et cum constet omnes ab omnibus impugnari, diverso tamen modo et ordine singuli laboramus.

Quamobrem ita nobis adversus haec arripienda sunt praelia, ut unusquisque vitium quo maxime infestatur exploret et adversus illud arripiat principale certamen. Unum namque nos ordinem praeliorum exercere debere nec de nosrta virtute confidere etiam legislator (Deut. VII) docet his verbis: Non timebis eos, quia Dominus Deus tuus in medio tui est, Deus magnus et terribilis. Ipse consumet nationes has in conspectu tuo paulatim atque per partes. Non poteris eas delere pariter, ne forte multiplicentur contra te bestiae terrae, dabitque eos Dominus Deus tuus in conspectu tuo, donec penitus deleantur. Sed neque debere nos in eorum extolli victoria similiter (Deut. VIII) monet: Ne postquam comederis, inquit, et satiatus fueris, domos pulchras aedificaveris et habitaveris in eis, habuerisque armenta et ovium greges, argenti et auri cunctarumque rerum copiam, elevetur cor tuum, et non reminiscaris Domini Dei tui, qui eduxit te de terra Aegypti, de domo servitutis, et ductor tuus fuit in solitudine magna atque terribili. Salomon quoque in Proverbiis (Prov. XXIV): Si ceciderit inimicus tuus, noli gratulari. In supplantatione autem ejus noli extolli. Ne videat Dominus ejus et avertat iram suam ab eo; id est, ne dispertias elationem cordis tui, ab ejus impugnatione discedet, et incipies, derelicturus ab eo, rursus ab illa quam per Dei gratiam superaveras passione vexari.

Quamobrem certos nos esse convenit, tam ipsis rerum quam innumeris Scripturarum testimoniis eruditos, nostris nos viribus, nisi solius Dei auxilio fulciamur, tantos hostes superare non posse, et ad ipsum quotidie summam victoriae nostrae referre debere. Ita super hoc quoque per Moysen (Deut. IX), Domino commonente: Ne dicas in corde tuo, cum deleverit eas Dominus Deus tuus in conspectu tuo: Propter justitiam meam introduxit me Dominus, ut terram hanc possiderem, cum propter impietates suas istae deletae sint nationes. Nec enim propter justitias tuas et aequitates cordis tui ingredieris ut possideas terram eorum, sed quia illae egerunt impie, te introeunte, deletae sunt. Rogo quid apertius potuit dici, vel cautius? Cum quanta cautela oportet nos esse!

Hae septem gentes, quarum terras egressis ex Aegypto filiis Israel daturum se Dominus repromittit. Quae omnia secundum Apostolum, cum in figura contigerint illis ad nostram commonitionem scripta (Deut. VII) debemus accipere.

Ita enim dicitur: Cum introduxerit te Dominus Deus in terram quam possessurus ingredieris et deleverit gentes multas coram te, Hethaeum, et Gergezaeum, et Amorrhaeum, Chananaeum, et Pherezaeum, et Jebusaeum, et Nevaeum, septem gentes multo majoris numeri quam tu es et robustiores te, tradideritque Dominus tibi eas, percutiesque eas usque ad internecionem.

Quod vero multo majoris numeri esse dicuntur, haec ratio est, quia plura sunt vitia quam virtutes. Et ideo in catalogo quidem dinumerantur septem gentes; in expugnatione vero earum sine numeri ascriptione ponuntur. Ita enim dicitur: Et deleverit gentes multas coram te. Numerosior est enim quam Israel carnalium passionum populus, qui de hoc septenario fomite vitiorum ac radice procedit, atque de octavo, qui notior est omnibus, regina, ut ita dicam, atque mater omnium vitiorum; ex his enim octo pullulant atque nascuntur hae filiae, id est, comessationes, ebrietates, turpiloquia, etc., superius descripta, quae commemorare perlongum est. Quae cum nobis levia judicentur, quid Apostolus de illis senserit (II Cor. X), vel quam super his sententiam tulerit, audiamus: Neque murmuraveritis, inquit, sicut quidam illorum murmuraverunt, et perierunt ab exterminatore. Et de tentatione: Neque tentemus Christum, sicut quidam eorum tentaverunt et a serpentibus perierunt. De detractione: Noli diligere detrahere, ne eradiceris; aliaque complura his similia. Quae cum sint multo majoris numeri quam virtutes, devictis tamen illis octo principalibus vitiis, ex quorum natura eas certum est emanare, omnes protinus conquiescunt, ac perpetua pariter cum eis internecione delentur.

Etenim quantum docet vetus traditio, has easdem terras Chananaeorum in quas introducuntur filii Israel, Sem filii Noe fuerant quondam, in orbis divisione, sortiti; quas deinceps per vim atque potentiam posteritas Cham persuasionis iniquitate possedit, in quo et Dei judicium rectissimum comprobatur. Qui et illos de locis alienis quae male occupaverant expulit, et istis antiquam patrum possessionem quae prosapiae eorum in divisione orbis fuerat deputata restituit. Quae figura in nobis quoque stare, certissima ratione cognoscitur. Nam voluntas Domini possessionem cordis nostri non vitiis, sed virtutibus naturaliter deputavit. Quae post praevaricationem Adae, insolescentibus vitiis, id est populis Chananaeis, a propria regione depulsae, cum ei rursum per Dei gratiam, diligentia nostra ac labore fuerint restitutae, non tam alienas occupasse terras quam proprias credendae sunt recepisse.

De hoc septenario fomite vitiorum Salomon quoque in Proverbiis ita describit (Prov. XXVI): Si te rogaverit inimicus voce magna, non consenseris ei, septem enim nequitiae sunt in anima ejus; id est, si gastrimargia te persuadet, ut relaxes corpori, quod continentiae decreveras modo, ne resolvas ejus subjectionem, quia confestim septem spiritus vitiorum aderunt tibi acriores quam illa passio quae primordiis fuerat superata, qui te mox ad deteriora pertrahant genera vitiorum. Quapropter Dominus per omnia est deprecandus, ut quod nostrae vires non habent ipsius misericordia succurrat.

The Scriptorium Project is the work of a small group of lay people of various apostolic churches who are interested in the preservation, transmission, and translation of the works of the early and medieval church. Our efforts are to make the works of the church fathers accessible to anyone who might have an interest in Christian antiquities and the theological, philosophical, and moral writings that have become the bedrock of Western Civilization.

To-date, our releases have pulled from the Greek, Syriac, Georgian, Latin, Celtic, Ethiopian, and Coptic traditions of Christianity, and have been pulled from sundry local traditions and languages.

Other Titles and Translations by D.P. Curtin:

Lebor Gabala Erenn by Nennius the Monk (2017)
The Eight Vices by Eutropis of Valencia (2017)
Three Letters from the Companion of the Bulgars by St. Rupert of Juvavum (2017)
Privileges of the Abbot of Canterbury by St. Augustine of Canterbury (2017)
Nicene Canons in the Old Nubian Language (2018)
Apology to Gunthamund, King of Vandals by Aemeilius Dracontius (2018)
First Book of Ethiopian Maccabees (2018)
Chronicon: a short chronicle of Visigothic Spain by Eutrandus of Ticino (2019)
Decrees of Aethelbert by St. Aethelbert, King of Kent (2019)
The Measure to be taxed for Penance by St. Columba of Iona (2019)
Protoevangelium of James: Greek and English Texts (2019)
Edicts of the Synod of Paris by Chlothar II, King of Franks (2019)
The Life of St. Desiderius by Sisebut, King of Visigoths (2019)
The Synod of Rome by St. Boniface IV of Rome (2019)
Letter to Pope Theodore by Victor of Carthage (2020)
The Decree of 610 by Gundemar, King of Visigoths (2020)
Laws of the Church by Chlothar III, King of Franks (2020)
Donations by St. Aethelbert, King of Kent (2020)
The Mystical Interpretation by St. Aileran the Wise (2020)
Laws of the Church by St. Dagobert II, King of Franks (2020)
The Old Nubian Miracle of St. Mena (2021)
About Fifteen Problems by St. Albertus Magnus (2022)
Testament of Some Former Things by John Scotus Eriugena (2022)
The Georgian Synaxarium (2022)
Instructions: Counsel for Novices by St. Ammonas the Hermit (2022)
The Syriac Menologium and Martyrology (2022)
Book on Religious Exercise and Quiet by St. Isaiah the Solitary (2022)
Vision of Theophilus by St. Cyril of Alexandria (2022)
On Fate (De Fato) by St. Albertus Magnus (2023)
Fragments of 'Chronicle' by Hippolytus of Thebes (2023)
Life of the Blessed Theotokos by Epiphanius Monachus (2023)
Syriac Life of John the Baptist by Serapion the Presbyter (2023)
Second Book of Ethiopian Maccabees (2023)

www.ingramcontent.com/pod-product-compliance
Lightning Source LLC
Chambersburg PA
CBHW070958120626
46546CB00004B/1681